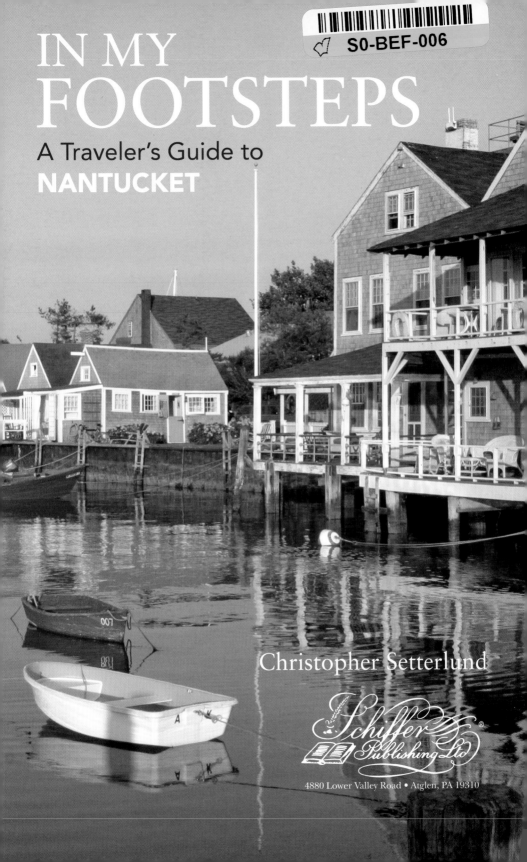

IN MY FOOTSTEPS

A Traveler's Guide to
NANTUCKET

Christopher Setterlund

Schiffer Publishing Ltd

4880 Lower Valley Road • Atglen, PA 19310

Other Schiffer books by Christopher Setterlund:
In My Footsteps: A Traveler's Guide to Martha's Vineyard, 978-0-7643-5019-1
In My Footsteps: A Cape Cod Travel Guide, 978-0-7643-4209-7

Cover design by John Cheek
Front cover photo © Michael Galvin.
Author image © Michael Jennings.
All other photographs © Christopher Setterlund
Type set in BauerBodni BT/Helvetica Neue LT Pro

ISBN: 978-0-7643-5094-8
Printed in China

Published by Schiffer Publishing, Ltd.
4880 Lower Valley Road
Atglen, PA 19310
Phone: (610) 593-1777; Fax: (610) 593-2002
E-mail: Info@schifferbooks.com
Web: www.schifferbooks.com

For our complete selection of fine books on this and related subjects, please visit our website at www.schifferbooks.com. You may also write for a free catalog.

Schiffer Publishing's titles are available at special discounts for bulk purchases for sales promotions or premiums. Special editions, including personalized covers, corporate imprints, and excerpts, can be created in large quantities for special needs. For more information, contact the publisher.

CONTENTS

V. Along Milestone Road, East to Siasconset   43

VI. Sankaty, Wauwinet, and Polpis   52

VII. From the Rotary Back to Downtown   63

INTRODUCTION

"You will realize the minute you set foot on our wharves, you have landed in a place back in time. This is a setting that begs you to relax and enjoy the simple pleasures that make our tiny island so unique. Join us . . . let our island come to life before your eyes, and create memories that will last a lifetime as you make Nantucket your own!"

— *PJ Martin-Smith, Executive Director Nantucket Chamber of Commerce.*

Thirty miles off the Cape Cod shore sits the quaint historic island of Nantucket. The name likely comes from the Wampanoag Tribe of Native Americans and translates as "faraway land." The first European settlers came to the island in 1621 when it was granted to the Plymouth Company of London. The island was purchased by Thomas Mayhew with the first true settlement beginning in 1659. Though the entire island is incorporated as the Town of Nantucket, there are a few small villages that add to the allure of this historic beauty.

Nantucket is known for its historic downtown area complete with cobblestone streets. The building and homes in the area have retained the charm of an eighteenth-century whaling village. Whaling was what Nantucket was known for above all else. It began around 1715 and lasted until around 1850. In that time Nantucket was the whaling capital of the world.

The island is a throwback to a simpler time, an image that Nantucket has worked hard to keep. There are numerous museums and historic homes all over the island but also countless wonderful restaurants and shops as well. It is the true definition of an island paradise. If you want to be a part of it, just pay this jewel a visit.

This tour takes you around the island, noting its world-renowned restaurants, museums, fabulous shops, and acres of conservation lands. You'll discover the historic homes, lighthouses, and beaches that make the island famous, but also some truly incredible locations only a local would know. I've divided the island into geographic regions for those who would like to expand the tour over several days, or you can take the tour from start to finish for a truly comprehensive overview of all Nantucket has to offer.

GETTING THERE

Take a ferry from Hyannis on the Cape, or fly in via Cape Air, either from Hyannis or one of the other airports that the airline serves. (Seasonal flights are also available on Jet Blue, Delta, US Airways, and United Airlines from a select number of airports; see NantucketAirport.com for details.)

THE STEAMSHIP AUTHORITY
69 South Street, Hyannis

For trips to Nantucket the Steamship Authority is a wonderful option. There are two types of ferries: the regular speed ferry that takes just over two hours but also carries vehicles, and the seasonal fast ferry that brings you dock to dock in about an hour. The Steamship ferries dock at 1 Steamboat Wharf in Nantucket. Schedules and fares change with the seasons; see SteamshipAuthority.com.

HY-LINE CRUISES
220 Ocean Street, Hyannis

This company's roots go back to when it was called Hyannis Harbor Tours in 1962. Hy-Line got its name in 1972 when Hyannis Harbor Tours bought out Nantucket Boat Company. Not only has Hy-Line been running ferries to Nantucket for decades but in 1988–89 they introduced first-class ferry travel as well. Hy-Line offers sixty-minute high-speed ferries to Nantucket from Hyannis on Cape Cod. The boats dock on Straight Wharf in Nantucket.

DOWNTOWN AND ITS NEARBY BEACHES

II

Our tour begins downtown. After arriving at one of the docks by ferry (or taking a cab or rental car to downtown from the airport if you flew in), the next step is finding a way to get around on the island. If you brought your own vehicle, then please proceed to the first location. If you came without one, you are in luck. There are a few ways to navigate Nantucket once you arrive. Here are two of them.

THE WAVE
NANTUCKET REGIONAL TRANSIT AUTHORITY

Begun in 1995 with only four vehicles as a way to alleviate the thick traffic on the island during the peak season, this service has grown exponentially. Today there are nine routes with thirteen buses. Buses for most routes run year-round from 7:00 a.m. to 11:30 p.m. Prices and schedules may be subject to change so it is always recommended to check the NRTA website: NRTAWave. com. The Wave's administrative offices are at 3 Chestnut Street, downtown.

YOUNG'S BICYCLE SHOP
6 Broad Street

A third-generation shop right off Steamboat Wharf, Young's is the oldest bike shop on the island. It was started in 1931 by Harvey Young. They have bikes for all ages and abilities including hybrids that are good for touring. Young's also rents cars, jeeps, and SUVs. Prices and availability of bikes and vehicles are always subject to change so it is best to check ahead by phone or their website: YoungsBicycleShop.com.

NANTUCKET BIKE SHOP
4 and 10 Broad Street

Another option with two locations on Steamboat Wharf is Nantucket Bike Shop, which rents both bikes and scooters. Check the website for information: NantucketBikeShop.com.

Now that your mode of transportation has been chosen it is time to see Nantucket, starting downtown and heading counterclockwise around the island.

1. ORAN MOR BISTRO & BAR
2 S. Beach Street

This is a highly regarded restaurant in the heart of downtown. At first glance this historic home appears to house only the studio of local artist Michael Gaillard. However, up a flight of stairs is the fabulously intimate Oran Mor. A large wine list, meticulously crafted and unique food, and a cozy atmosphere come together to create one of the top-rated bistros on Nantucket. Spread across three rooms, this spot owned by Chef Chris Freeman and his wife, Heather, is perfect for friends, family, or a special night out for two.

GPS: 41.287365, -70.098656

Directions: From Oran Mor, continue on S. Beach Street to the next destination on the right. (Distance: 500 feet; Driving Time: <1 min.)

2. LOLA 41
15 S. Beach Street

Part sushi restaurant, part bistro, and part high-class bar, this spot has distinct allure. There is something for all food connoisseurs here, even those who do not enjoy sushi. The gravy fries are life changing and a must. Intimate and dimly lit, Lola 41 has a style all its own that makes it stand out among a multitude of distinctive establishments. With top reviews from Zagat, *New York Times Magazine* and others, this spot is well known far from the island's shores.

3. THE WHITE ELEPHANT HOTEL
50 Easton Street

Within sight of the famed Brant Point Lighthouse sits this sixty-seven-room historic luxury hotel. Established in the 1920s as a project of noted Nantucket socialite Elizabeth Ludwig, the White Elephant has undergone extensive changes over the years. During the 1960s, some of the original building was dismantled and moved, becoming summer housing known as the Garden Cottages for employees. Today, it has all the amenities of a twenty-first century posh luxury hotel with a touch of the old seaside escape of the 1920s.

4. BRANT POINT COAST GUARD STATION/OLD BRANT POINT LIGHTHOUSE
Easton Street

Only a few hundred feet from the current Brant Point Lighthouse stands the Brant Point Coast Guard Station and the last Brant Point Lighthouse. The tower, without a lantern, was erected in 1856 and decommissioned in 1901 when shifting sands created the need for a new lighthouse

on the point. The headless lighthouse base is now used by the Coast Guard as a radio room and office. In addition to the Coast Guard buildings and old Brant Point Lighthouse, you'll find a pair of wooden triangular structures. These are the Nantucket Harbor Range Lighthouses built in 1908. They help guide vessels through the narrow channel into Nantucket Harbor. For an unknown reason, the structure closest to the street is known as Nantucket Reef Range Front Light.

GPS: 41.289916, -70.090376

Directions: From the Coast Guard Station continue on Easton Street a few hundred feet to the end. The next destination is straight ahead.

5. BRANT POINT LIGHTHOUSE
Easton Street

This is one of the most visited and photographed lighthouses in the country. Known for its diminutive stature and railed walkway, Brant Point Lighthouse sits at the mouth of Nantucket Harbor where the ferries pass by. The current Brant Point Lighthouse is actually the tenth light and the seventh tower near that spot. It was erected in 1901 and became a popular design, as there are replicas of Brant Point Lighthouse on Lewis Bay in Hyannis, Massachusetts, and at the Mystic Seaport in Mystic, Connecticut. The actual Brant Point gets its name from the small arctic goose that used to migrate to the area during the summer in the early days of the Nantucket settlement.

GPS: 41.296137, -70.104666

Directions: From Brant Point head back down Easton Street, then turn right onto Hulbert Street. Follow it 0.7 miles, turn right onto Bathing Beach Road, then follow it to the end. (Distance: 0.9 miles; Driving Time: 3 mins.)

6. JETTIES BEACH
Bathing Beach Road

At the mouth of Nantucket Harbor, this is a popular spot right off the ferry. It is a beautiful and unique spot thanks to the long breakwater (jetty) that sticks out into the ocean. This also keeps the water calm, which adds to the allure of this beach.

There are concession stands in season, but if that is not your thing, Jetties Beach Bar & Restaurant is located a short walk off the sand with a larger menu. You'll also find playground, tennis courts, and volleyball nets.

7. NANTUCKET CLIFF RANGE LIGHTHOUSES & "THE SHOE" COTTAGE
Pawguvet Lane

Tucked away behind the Jetties Beach tennis courts are three intriguing pieces of Nantucket history. The Nantucket Range Lighthouses on this property were two of several diminutive lighthouses, called "bug lights" by the locals, along the Nantucket coast. These two particular lighthouses were discontinued in 1912. The lighthouses were named "Mic" and "Cyc" after *Mike and Ike,* the popular comic strip that debuted in 1907. Cyc is the taller lighthouse; the shorter Mic is behind the cottage. The signs with these names still hang on the wooden buildings today.

Nantucket Range Lighthouse "Cyc"

In between the small wooden structures sits a cottage named "The Shoe." The cottage was originally owned by the Gilbreth family about whom *Cheaper By the Dozen* was written in 1948. They purchased the two lighthouses that sit on the property and actually used them as rooms for the children as the "Shoe" cottage was not big enough for all of them.

"The Shoe" Cottage

8. CLIFFSIDE BEACH CLUB
Jefferson Avenue

This is every bit the "island" resort. There are only twenty-two rooms, nearly all with a panoramic view of the private beach between Steps and Jetties Beaches. The tropical feel is enhanced when you can step out of your room directly onto the soft sand. The oldest structures on the grounds date back to the early 1900s, including the lobby, which has been renovated while keeping the charm. One of the most popular resorts on the island, it is frequented by people of celebrity status but they mix right in with the average traveler. Stay for a night and grab a drink at the neighboring Galley Beach restaurant and bar.

GPS: 41.293936, -70.109777
Directions: From Cliffside head down Jefferson Avenue, then turn right onto Cobblestone Hill. Take the first right onto Lincoln Avenue. Follow it 0.1 miles to the next destination on the right. (Distance: .4 miles; Driving Time: 1 min.)

9. STEPS BEACH
Indian Avenue

A beautifully secret locale, Steps Beach is hard to find and harder to leave. You must look for the stone with "Welcome to Steps Beach" engraved on it; there is a narrow pathway with racks for bikes along the way. Once into the open space, the view is simply breathtaking. There is a stairway leading down to the sand. To the right is a beach shack named "Le Shack." To the left is the sandy path over the dunes to the water. The views are every bit the story as the beach itself. No lifeguard, no restrooms, no concessions.

III

FROM DOWNTOWN, WEST TO MADAKET

GPS: 41.289799,-70.107216

Directions: From Steps Beach head down Lincoln Ave., follow it 0.2 miles, then turn right onto Highland Avenue. Turn left onto Cliff Road, then follow it 0.1 miles to the next destination on the right. (Distance: .4 miles, Driving Time: 2 mins.)

1. SOMETHING NATURAL
50 Cliff Road

Only a short distance from downtown, this is one of the top-rated eateries on the island and for good reason. There is no shortage of tremendous choices for sandwiches, which you can have on your choice of eight kinds of freshly baked bread. Have some award-winning cookies, or purchase some merchandise to remember the trip. When the weather cooperates, make sure to sit outside at the picnic tables to get the full experience.

2. TUPANCY LINKS
Cliff Road

Blink and you might miss the entrance to this conservation land located along the Cliff Road bike path. It is named for the family who donated the property: Sallie Gail and Oswald Tupancy. This open space of seventy-three acres was formerly a nine-hole golf course. There is a small parking area, and a short walk up a trail leads to an amazing view of the north shore of the island. Trails lead you past some of the old golf course holes; it is possible to see the outlines of the old greens.

GPS: 41.292685, -70.137821

Directions: From Tupancy Links keep going west on Cliff Road 0.3 miles, then turn right onto Washing Pond Rd., follow it 0.5 miles to a dirt road that veers right. Follow it to the end. (Distance: 0.9 miles; Driving Time: 5 mins.)

3. CAPAUM POND
Washing Pond Road

So close to the ocean, this pond is on the north side of the island almost halfway between Jetties Beach and Eel Point. It is a little off the beaten path with no markings on the dirt road that leads to this remarkable setting. This spot was at one point a harbor until a storm in 1717 deposited the sand that now comprises the tiny barrier separating pond from ocean. This is a wonderful lesser-known Nantucket location that needs to be enjoyed and explored.

GPS: 41.285912, -70.131721

Directions: From Capaum Pond head back out on the dirt road to Washing Pond Road, and follow it back out to Cliff Road. Turn immediately left onto W. Chester Street. There will be a sign marked "Historic Cemetery" and also a path leading up a hill to the left. (Distance: 0.7 miles; Driving Time: 5 mins.)

4. FOUNDERS BURIAL GROUND & MAXCY'S POND
Cliff Road

This is one of the most difficult places to find on the island, and it is also one of the most worthwhile. The Founders Cemetery is located off Cliff Road and then off another dirt road. It overlooks Maxcy's Pond.

The cemetery has two large stone markers listing the names of the original settlers of the island. There is a replica of the stone of John Gardner, one of the original settlers, here as well; the original stone sits at the Nantucket Historical Association. The first mentions of a "forefathers burial ground" date back to 1838. It is an unassuming yet awe-inspiring area when considering the history of Nantucket lies before you.

Maxcy's Pond, which lies behind the burial ground, has a name the history of which is as difficult to find as the Founders Burial Ground itself. The Maxcy name first appears on maps in 1821. The pond was originally called Wyer's Pond as it abutted the Wyer family property. The reason for the name change has been impossible to find so far.

QUAKER BURIAL GROUND
ON THIS SITE THE SECOND MEETING HOUSE FOR
ISLAND QUAKERS WAS BUILT AND USED FOR
WORSHIP UNTIL 1792
IN THE MAJOR SECTION OF THIS CEMETERY
ARE INTERRED THE THOUSANDS OF ORTHODOX
FRIENDS NOTED FOR THEIR BELIEF THAT GRAVE
STONES WERE A PART OF IDOLATRY.
THE FEW MARKERS IN THIS PLOT WERE
PLACED BY THE HICKSITE AND GURNYITE
QUAKERS, KNOWN BY THE EARLIER GROUP
AS HERETICAL FRIENDS

GPS: 41.289493, -70.150540)

Directions: From the Founders Burial Ground, turn left (west) onto Cliff Road, then bear right onto Eel Point Road. After 0.7 miles turn right onto Dionis Beach Road and follow it to the end. (Distance: 1.3 miles; Driving Time: 5 mins.)

5. DIONIS BEACH
& DIONIS BEACH BIKE PATH
Dionis Beach Road

A small beach located almost exactly in the middle of the north shore, Dionis Beach can be easy to miss while driving. You must keep your eyes open for the white stone with "Dionis Beach" painted on it. It is named for Dionis Stevens Coffin, who settled on Nantucket in 1659 with her husband Tristram. At one point during the 1880s, there was an attempted summer colony in the area called Dionis City.

The beach is small but has a unique pathway to the water that is lined with conch shells atop the beach fences. There are good-sized dunes that shelter the beach some, and it is less crowded than those closer to downtown.

- Lifeguards in season.
- Restrooms.
- No concessions, but there are vending machines.

GPS: 41.292435, -70.170055

Directions: From Dionis Beach head back to Eel Point Road, then turn right. Follow it 1.1 miles to the next destination on the left. (Distance: 1.3 miles; Driving Time: 7 mins.)

6. LINDA LORING NATURE FOUNDATION
Eel Point Road

Established in 1999, this 270-acre conservation area shows that Nantucket is much more than simply miles of pristine beaches. Centered on Eel Point Road within sight of said beaches, this preserve was founded by Linda Loring. Beginning in 1957 she purchased land in the area piece by piece over the span of forty-two years. Refusing to sell or develop on the land, she eventually created the Nature Foundation as it stands today.

The preserve contains pitch pine forest, scrub pine forest, and the endangered heathlands and sandplain grasslands. In the future, the Nature Foundation plans to create a scenic trail network and a LEED-certified (green) nature facility, complete with classrooms. It is a perfect chance to see more of the natural beauty of the island while never being far from the waves.

GPS: 41.291061, -70.192325

Directions: From the Nature Foundation continue on Eel Point Road heading west. Follow it 1.2 miles to the next destination. (Distance: 1.2 miles, Driving Time: 8 mins.)

7. EEL POINT
Eel Point Road

One of the first properties acquired by the Nantucket Conservation Foundation, Eel Point is a very secluded area in the northwest corner of the island. A sandy road leads to this 100-acre property and the sandy paths continue all through the property. This is a beautiful area to lose yourself in the unspoiled magnificence of Nantucket. It is a haven for shorebirds and includes amazing views to the west of Madaket Harbor. There is a small parking area near the entrance. Eel Point is a great walking or hiking area with seemingly endless dunes and small ponds. Eel Point Beach is just over 0.25 miles from the parking area.

GPS: 41.281055, -70.192366

Directions: From Eel Point, continue south on Eel Point Road, then bear right onto Warrens Landing and follow it 0.7 miles. Turn right onto Madaket Road, follow it 0.9 miles, turn right onto North Cambridge Street. Follow it 0.4 miles to the next destination. (Distance: 2.5 miles; Driving Time: 9 mins.)

8. SETTLER'S LANDING
Blue Heron Way

This is a beautiful little overlook that might be missed by most visitors to the island. There is a spectacular view of Madaket Harbor, and you can walk down to the water. There is also a stone marker near the stairs erected in 2009 that celebrates 350 years from when the Wampanoag Tribe of Native Americans first met the original English settlers. It is a peaceful little stop on the way to the more well-known beaches.

9. MADAKET BEACH
Madaket Road

A popular beach in the southwestern corner of the island, Madaket Beach and the surrounding village once had so many different spellings that it caused the Board on Geographic Names to designate its official spelling in 1966. It is a great spot for surfing and sunsets. Though parking is limited there is ample room along the sand if you have an off-road vehicle.

The name "Madaket" is thought to possibly be related to the Algonquin words meaning "land without wood." This is backed up by the fact that when the settlers spent their first winter on Nantucket in 1659 they chose to spend it farther east toward the center of the island rather than this area due to the lack of trees.

- Limited parking
- Lifeguards in season.
- Restrooms.

GPS: 1.272188, -70.203684

Directions: From Madaket Beach turn left onto Ames Avenue for the next destination. (Distance: 0.2 miles; Driving Time: 1 min.)

10. MILLIE'S BRIDGE & HITHER CREEK
Ames Avenue

This spot feels like the gateway to another world. A beautiful wooden bridge spans a creek (though it's more like a river), and the place is packed with boats during the summer. Millie's Bridge is the entrance to Smith's Point and stands close to 200 feet long. It crosses over Hither Creek, which got its name as part of a pair of creeks at Madaket Harbor; Further Creek was the other one. Hither Creek was closer to downtown, as it lay on the east end of the harbor. Further Creek was destroyed by Hurricane Esther in 1961. This also created Esther Island, which has since reconnected to the mainland. The creek is seasonally home to birds such as egrets.

The bridge is named for iconic Madaket resident Millie Jewett. She would greet visitors and sell ice cream from her yard, which was on Hither Creek. She earned the highest civilian rank from the Coast Guard, thanks to her work caring for the beaches and patrolling for shipwrecks.

11. SMITH'S POINT
Ames Avenue

This spot at the southwestern corner of Nantucket is a hidden gem worth the drive. Passing Madaket Beach and heading west leads you over Hither Creek across Millie's Bridge and into a quiet village filled with beach shacks, larger homes, sandy, sometimes impassible roads, and an array of beautiful beaches and coastal charm.

It is named Smith's Point for one of the early Smiths who settled Nantucket. It could be either John Smith, who partnered with original Nantucket settler Thomas Mayhew in 1659, or Richard Smith, who was an artisan who came to the island in 1661. Smith's Point is also notable for being near the beach where Native Americans would come ashore when crossing from Martha's Vineyard.

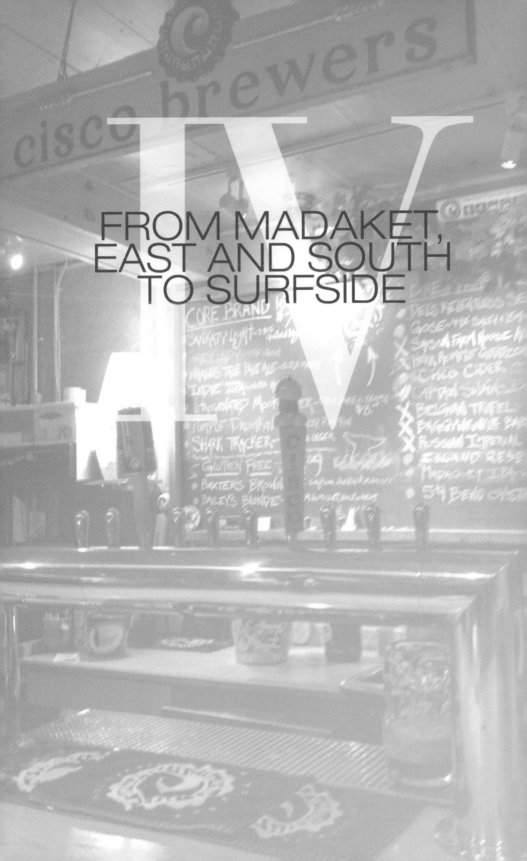

IV

FROM MADAKET, EAST AND SOUTH TO SURFSIDE

GPS: 41.284026, -70.170194
Directions: From Smith's Point head back out to Madaket Road, turn left (east) and follow it 1.9 miles to the next destination on the right. (Distance: 2.2 miles, Driving Time: 5 mins.)

1. THE GUT
Madaket Road

A pretty scenic turnoff, the Gut is a narrow piece of land that separates Long Pond from the North Head of Long Pond. There is a nice dock to fish from on the southern side of Madaket Road, which passes over. This location is passed by many every day; there is a dirt turn-off where a few cars can park. The ponds are great for small boats and other non-motorized vessels.

2. ABIAH FOLGER MEMORIAL FOUNTAIN
76 Madaket Road

As you continue along Madaket Road, slow down or you might miss this historic location. Abiah Folger might not be a household name until her famous offspring is mentioned: Ms. Folger was the mother of Benjamin Franklin. She married Josiah Franklin in 1689. Her family's farm was once located not far from the fountain memorial. It was erected by the National Society Daughters of the American Revolution in 1900. It is possible that she is also related to J. A. Folger, creator of Folgers Coffee. He was also born on Nantucket.

3. CISCO BREWERY

Bartlett Farm Road

A top destination for lovers of fine alcoholic beverages, Cisco Brewers was founded in 1992. Cisco Brewers then connected with the Nantucket Vineyard, which was formed in 1981. Together they are the Triple Eight Distillery, found in the quiet solitude of the central part of the island. There are tours of the brewery with or without tastings of the fine wines, spirits, and, of course, craft beers. The wines, which use grapes imported from California, Washington, and New York, are currently sold only on the island. The beers, however, can be found in other locations throughout New England and as far away as Florida and Georgia.

There is also a cozy bar where visitors can sit and enjoy many of the beers and spirits while listening to live music. It is a great place to stop while passing through, or a way to finish a long day of fun in the sun.

The Cisco name comes from New York banker John Jay Cisco, who built a summer home at the end of Hummock Pond Road on what is now Cisco Beach in the 1860s. The beach itself is a former whaling station.

GPS: 41.244172, -70.094785

Directions: From Cisco Brewery head left back out to Hummock Pond Road. Turn right on Hummock Pond, follow it 0.5 miles, turn right onto Somerset Lane and follow it 0.5 miles, then turn left onto Somerset Road. Bear right onto Marble Way, which quickly merges into Bartlett Road. After 0.8 miles turn right onto Surfside Road, and follow it to the end, where the next destination is located. (Distance: 4.1 miles, Driving Time: 14 mins.)

4. SURFSIDE BEACH

Surfside Road

A straight shot south from downtown, this is one of the most popular beaches on the island. It is located near the airport and can have some great waves. It is wonderful for activities like kite surfing, though not on the eastern side of the beach near the airport. There is a large area for bike parking. The beach itself is set back from the road with a sandy pathway to the shore. The beach is very large, having room for new arrivals on even the most crowded days.

The Surfside village was begun in the 1880s as an investment by Charles and Henry Coffin in hopes of selling lots to their mainland relatives. At one point a railroad ran from downtown to Surfside. The Coffin brothers went bankrupt when very few lots were sold, and the railroad tracks were torn up to make tanks for World War I.

- Lifeguards in season.
- Restrooms.
- Concessions available in season.

V

ALONG MILESTONE ROAD, EAST TO SIASCONSET

GPS: 41.265449, -70.032125

Directions: From Surfside Beach head back up Surfside Road. Follow it 1.1 miles, then turn right onto Fairgrounds Road and follow it 0.9 miles, then turn left onto Old South Road. After 0.1 miles, at the rotary take the first exit for Milestone Road. Follow it 2 to 3 miles for the next destination. (Distance: 5 miles, Driving Time: 11 mins.)

1. MIDDLE MOORS SERENGETI & MILESTONE BIKE PATH

Milestone Road

Alongside the Milestone Road bike path is a site that looks like an African landscape. A serengeti is a land area with low-growing vegetation mixed with occasional trees; Nantucket's serengeti makes up roughly 400 acres of the 3,200 acres of conservation land on the island. To further enhance the experience there are wild animal cutouts scattered across the landscape. This wonder in the center of Nantucket can be enjoyed by hikers, or even those just passing by on a bicycle heading east or west.

The Milestone Road Bike Path is 6 miles long and runs from the Milestone rotary into the center of the village of Siasconset, on the island's eastern shores. The bike path also goes past a large cranberry bog with Sankaty Head Lighthouse visible across the valley. It is a relatively flat ride and a great way to enjoy the middle of Nantucket.

GPS: 41.261265,-69.964159

Directions: From the Middle Moors Serengeti follow Milestone Road to the village of Siasconset, where the name changes to Main Street. Keep going to the 'Sconset rotary, then turn right onto Ocean Avenue and quickly bear left onto Gully Road to arrive at the next destination. (Distance: 3.7 miles, Driving Time: 6 mins.)

2. 'SCONSET FOOTBRIDGE
Gully Road

Thousands of visitors to Nantucket pass underneath this piece of history each year, and many probably pay it no attention. The ninety-foot wooden bridge was developed by local architect Charles H. Robinson in 1873. The bridge connected the Sunset Heights neighborhood with the village of Siasconset to make travel easier for citizens of each location. From the bridge, there is a breathtaking view of nearby Siasconset Beach to the east. It is easy to park your car, or bike, and sit up on the bridge taking in the birds-eye view of the scenery.

The village of Siasconset (also known affectionately as 'Sconset) was developed in the late 1800s as a summer resort. Famed actors of the time, including Joseph Jefferson, DeWolf Hopper, and Frank Gilmore, visited during the season, as did Henry David Thoreau in 1854.

3. 'SCONSET BEACH
Gully Road

This beach sits on the eastern tip of the island and is very popular with those staying in this summer resort village. It is an easy ride along the Milestone Bike path, or by shuttle if one doesn't have a car. The beach itself is a long stretch, making it possible to find a nice section of sand to call your own even in the busiest of summer months. It is within sight of the 'Sconset Footbridge, and the view of the beach from there is amazing.

- Lifeguards in season.
- Restrooms within walking distance.

GPS: 41.262344,-69.963861

Directions: From 'Sconset Beach head back up Gully Road, and at the rotary take the first right onto Elbow Lane. Continue onto Broadway. The next destination is a few hundred feet up on the left. (Distance: 0.2 miles, Driving Time: 1 min.)

4. MICAH COFFIN HOUSE, A.K.A. AULD LANG SYNE

6 Broadway

This is one of many historic homes along Broadway in the village of 'Sconset. Auld Lang Syne, as this fishing shack is known, is arguably the oldest structure on Nantucket. Built in the 1670s, it was originally a small rectangular dwelling owned by Micah Coffin. He paid local Native Americans to fish for him while he stayed onshore to cook their bounty. The shack has had additions but it retains that classic seventeenth-century feel.

5. NAUMA COTTAGE
27 Broadway

With a name meaning "Long Point," Nauma is one of the many beautiful homes and cottages along 'Sconset's historic Broadway, though it is believed to have been moved there from another locale. History shows it may have been moved from nearby Sesachacha Pond, with the barn attached to the cottage brought to this site in 1868 from the village of Shimmo.

6. 'SCONSET BLUFF WALK
Bank Street

A not-so-secret secret spot in 'Sconset is the Bluff Walk. The entrance is on the curve of Bank Street up a short hill. At the top is a marvelous scenic route with the backyards of beautiful homes on your left and the ocean below the bluff to the right. This is a public way, but it is important to stay on the path and be respectful of people's property. The mile-long "path" leads you eventually to Sankaty Head Lighthouse. This hidden gem has very rarely ever caused a problem for the property owners whose yards run alongside it. It is a more up-close and personal version of Newport's Cliff Walk. Please note there is no real parking for this; it might be better to park elsewhere and walk to it.

VI

SANKATY, WAUWINET, AND POLPIS

GPS: 41.283192,-69.965057

Directions: From the Bluff Walk head back out to the rotary via Codfish Park Road, which becomes Gully Road. At the rotary take the first right onto Elbow Lane; this becomes Broadway. Follow Broadway straight out to Shell Street. Take the first right onto Butterfly Lane, which will become Baxter Road. Follow Baxter 1.1 miles to its end and the next destination. (Distance: 2 miles, Driving Time: 7 mins.)

1. SANKATY HEAD LIGHTHOUSE
Baxter Road

Taking its name from the Wampanoag word for "Cool Hill" Sankaty is a very unique lighthouse. Nestled against the Sankaty Head Golf Course, this red-and-white striped tower caps an amazing view of the area. Able to be seen from miles inland on the 'Sconset Bike Path, Sankaty Head was built in 1850. It was reportedly New England's most powerful lighthouse, with its light visible up to forty miles away. In 2007, due to erosion, the lighthouse was moved to a location 280 feet away from the bluffs. Near the entrance to the grounds of the lighthouse is the highest point on Nantucket at 111 feet above sea level.

GPS: 41.304101, -69.979209)

Directions: From Sankaty Head Lighthouse, head back down Baxter Road, and after 0.5 miles turn right onto Bayberry Lane, then turn right onto Sankaty Road. This becomes Polpis Road; follow Polpis 2.7 miles, then turn right onto Quidnet Road. Follow it 1.1 miles, then turn right onto Sesachacha Road. Follow Sesachacha 0.2 miles to the next destination on the right. (Distance: 4.8 miles, Driving Time: 11 mins.)

2. SESACHACHA POND & WILDLIFE SANCTUARY
Sesachacha Road

This is the largest brackish pond on the island. This means there is a mix of salt and fresh water. The pond is 250 acres in size and sits very close to Quidnet Beach. In the seventeenth century Native Americans had a village around the pond. The village of Quidnet, which lies north of the pond, was once land surrounded by water. In fact, the Quidnet name comes from the Algonquin word *aquidnet*, meaning "at the island." The pond is a part of the larger Sesachacha Heathlands Wildlife Sanctuary, which measures 875 acres in size and is home at times to 300 different species of birds.

GPS: 41.302603, -70.010980

Directions: From the pond follow Sesachacha Road back to Quidnet Road. Turn left on Quidnet and follow it 1.1 miles. Turn right onto Polpis Harbor Road and follow it to the next destination. (Distance: 2 miles, Driving Time: 7 mins.)

3. POLPIS HARBOR
Polpis Harbor Road

Only slightly off the beaten path is this spot that mixes beautiful scenery with history. Polpis Harbor sits at the end of a dirt road and is a calm, serene spot to keep one's boat. It is shielded from the ocean by the Coatue peninsula, which stretches from Great Point six miles all the way down to the mouth of Nantucket Harbor. To the west of the parking area is a series of walking trails that leads you around and over a salt marsh and the remnants of Holly Farm. The rows of holly trees are all that remains today.

The village of Polpis was originally a Native American settlement. Its land was purchased for farming by the first settlers in the mid-seventeenth century. In 1851 the ship *British Queen* wrecked in the Muskeget Channel, which flows in between Nantucket and Martha's Vineyard. Fleeing from the potato famine in Ireland on their way to New York, most survivors continued that course. Robert and Julia Mooney stayed on Nantucket in Polpis as tenant farmers.

GPS: 41.330388, -69.997155

Directions: From Polpis Harbor turn left onto Wauwinet Road, and follow it 2.4 miles to the next destination. (Distance: 2.4 miles, Driving Time: 8 mins.)

4. COSKATA-COATUE WILDLIFE REFUGE
Wauwinet Road

There are more than 1,100 acres of pristine woodland and beach here. An off-road vehicle and permit are a must to explore the seemingly endless miles of beaches. It is a haven for fishing and hunting as well as bird watching. Two thin peninsulas of land make up this natural gem, coming together at Great Point. This spot boasts a lighthouse and is owned by the Nantucket Conservation Foundation. At some points, the land is so narrow that it is possible to see erosion causing a breach in the sand; eventually, Great Point will become an island.

In addition to the expected plant and animal finds here it is also possible to find cacti and snowy owls while driving along the sand. The name "Coskata" is Wampanoag for "at the broad woods," while "Coatue" could mean "at the pine woods," though this is not as clearly known. Set aside a good amount of time to give this area a proper viewing.

Note: Off-road vehicle permits are required here. As of 2015, off-island vehicles: $140.

GPS: 41.390085, -70.048264
Directions: From here it is an off-road journey for approximately 5 miles over soft sand to the next destination. Remember to deflate your tires for better traction before attempting this part of the trip. (Distance: 5 miles, Driving Time: Approximately 20 mins.)

5. GREAT POINT LIGHTHOUSE
Wauwinet Road

One of the most remote lighthouses in the country sits at the end of a seven-mile stretch of sand known as Great Point, a part of the Coskata-Coatue Wildlife Refuge. An off-road vehicle and permit are a must (see the previous entry) but the trip out is worth it to stand before this stone giant. The current lighthouse, built in 1986, is the third one on the spot. The seventy-foot tall structure is visible for miles around including places like Jetties Beach, where it appears like a white matchstick on the horizon. It was automated in the 1950s and has stood alone on Great Point ever since the keeper's house burned down in 1966. There are tours to the lighthouse seasonally. It is possibly as far as one can get from civilization on the island.

GPS: 41.296258, -70.015655

Directions: From the lighthouse head back through the sandy trails to Wauwinet Road. There is a spot to air up your tires just after the dirt road becomes paved again on the right side. Follow Wauwinet Road all the way, then bear right onto Polpis Road. Follow it 0.4 miles to the next destination on the right. (Distance: 5.5 miles, Driving Time: 21 mins.)

6. OLD POLPIS CEMETERY
Polpis Road

This spot is as important for what is not seen as for what is seen. This cemetery appears as an unassuming patch of green along Polpis Road with only a white sign marking its entrance. Upon further inspection there are only a scant six gravestones sitting atop the crest of the cemetery's hill, none older than 1990. However, this cemetery is as old as the first settlements in Polpis, which date back to the 1660s. It even contained the stones of the Swain family, who were some of the original settlers of the area.

It is a mystery as to where the much older historic stone markers have gone. As late as 2010 there were purportedly many more markers here; now the only thing that gives a clue to what lies below are odd circular-shaped objects in perfect rows along the grass. It is an interesting and peculiar spot.

GPS: 41.281453, -70.024935

Directions: From the cemetery continue west along Polpis Road for 1.1 miles. Turn left onto Altar Rock Road, which is a dirt road. Follow it 0.7 miles to the next destination. (Distance: 1.8 miles; Driving Time: 7 mins.)

7. ALTAR ROCK
Altar Rock Road

One of the highest elevations on the island and with a spectacular panoramic view, this is a must-see located in Middle Moors. At more than 100 feet above sea level, from this vantage point one can see most of the island including Great Point Light and Sankaty Head Light. There are several dirt roads leading through the Moors, which makes getting around the area easier and a bit adventurous. Not far from Altar Rock is a round building with a needle-top. This is a navigational aid used by aircraft on their final approach to the airport two miles away.

8. NANTUCKET SHIPWRECK & LIFESAVING MUSEUM
Fulling Mill Road

On an historic whaling, fishing, and shipping island such as Nantucket this is a necessary and must-see location. The island has been dubbed the "graveyard of the Atlantic" due to the more than 700 shipwrecks in the waters surrounding Nantucket since the nineteenth century. There are numerous guided tours daily, in season, showcasing more than 5,000 objects from famous shipwrecks, full-sized vessels, and beautiful artwork. Outside of the museum sits the third-order lantern from Great Point Lighthouse, which was placed atop the lighthouse in 1857.

This is a great family-friendly outing and essential for anyone who enjoys nautical history. It sits on a marsh overlooking Nantucket Harbor and is an easy ride on the Polpis Bike Path or via the NRTA shuttle. The museum is open from Memorial Day through Columbus Day. Admission: adults, $6; children, ages 5–17, $4; children under 5, free.

FROM THE ROTARY
BACK TO DOWNTOWN

GPS: 41.271049,-70.091873

Directions: From the museum continue west on Old Polpis Road and then Polpis Road. After 2.5 miles bear right onto Milestone Road. At the rotary take the second exit for Sparks Avenue, and follow it 0.2 miles to the next destination on the left. (Distance: 3.0 miles; Driving Time: 7 mins.)

1. DOWNYFLAKE DOUGHNUTS
18 Sparks Ave.

Just outside of the thumping downtown area, this restaurant is a must for breakfast lovers. Famous for their blueberry pancakes with blueberry syrup, Downyflake has been an island staple since 1935. The original doughnut shop was located downtown and the current establishment is believed to be the last remaining outpost of that franchise; at one point in the 1940s and 1950s there were dozens of Downyflake Doughnut shops across America. It maintains a comfortable old-school vibe even today with great food and affordable prices.

2. AFRICAN-AMERICAN MEETING HOUSE

29 York Street

This is a monumental piece of Nantucket and American history. This small, unassuming wooden building is the only public structure built and occupied by the island's African Americans during the nineteenth century. It was originally built in 1827 and was a church, a school for young children, and a meeting house. Schools on Nantucket were not integrated until 1847; when this occurred, the building became the Pleasant Street Baptist Church. It was restored and reopened in 1999. It is open year-round but by appointment during the colder months. Admission: adults, $5; seniors and children, ages 13–17, $3; children under 12, free.

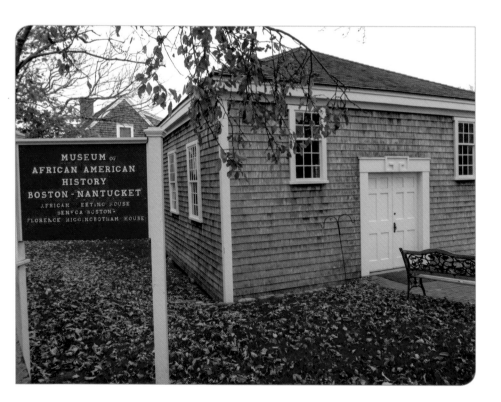

3. THE OLD MILL
50 Prospect Street

Overlooking Mill Hill Park and some other beautiful scenery sits the oldest working mill in the United States. Only a short walk or drive from downtown, this mill was built in 1746 by Nathan Wilbur, who was familiar with the "smock" mill from his time in Holland. At one point there were five such smock mills on the island; this is the only one that has survived. It was nearly torn down in the early nineteenth century, but was sold in 1828 for $20 to Jared Gardner, who chose to restore it rather than dismantle it. The mill is open daily from late May through mid-October. Admission: adults, $6; children, $3.

4. MARIA MITCHELL HOUSE & OBSERVATORY

Vestal Street

One of the most famed residents of historic Nantucket was Maria Mitchell, the very first female astronomer. Her home and observatory are two of the most important places in US women's history. The Mitchell House on the corner of Vestal Street was built in 1790 and became the home of the Mitchell family in 1818, the year Maria was born. She discovered a comet in 1847 and received a gold medal from the King of Denmark. Mitchell was widely sought after in the years following her discovery and was the first female librarian at the Nantucket Atheneum.

The Vestal Street Observatory, diagonally across from the Mitchell House, has been used as a site for research and lectures since its erection in 1908. It is recognizable by its brick façade and observation dome roof. There is also another observatory located nearby on Milk Street with stargazing available on appropriate nights.

The Mitchell House is open for tours from mid-June through Labor Day and on a reduced schedule from Labor Day through Columbus Day. It is a great spot for families and lovers of astronomy.

GPS: 41.281185, -70.103298

Directions: From the Mitchell House head back out on Vestal Street, and turn left onto Milk Street. When you reach the intersection with Main Street the next destination is on the left. (Distance: 0.1 miles; Driving Time: 1 min.)

5. CHRISTOPHER STARBUCK HOUSE
Main Street

A short walk away from downtown Nantucket is one of the oldest homes on the island. Though Nantucket boasts more than 800 pre-Civil War homes, the Starbuck House was originally erected in 1690 and is one of the few seventeenth-century homes remaining here. It has been relatively unaltered since it was fully completed in 1757. The original east end of the house was purported to have been moved to the Main Street location from Shelburne, which was the first settlement on Nantucket's north shore. The layout of the home is diagonal, which aligns it with the old street lines and lends credence to the theory that the house was moved.

The house sits in Monument Square, a one-time thriving hub of downtown before the settlement began moving closer to the harbor in the late nineteenth century. The monument itself, which creates a sort of unofficial rotary, is dedicated to the memeory of men who died in the Civil War.

GPS: 41.287951, -70.106441

Directions: From the Starbuck House head down Gardner Street, which becomes Liberty Street and then N. Liberty Street. Follow N. Liberty 0.5 mile, and turn right onto Sunset Hill Lane. After 0.1 miles the next destination is on the left. (Distance: 0.6 miles; Driving Time: 2 mins.)

6. JETHRO COFFIN HOUSE, A.K.A. "OLDEST HOUSE"

Sunset Hill Lane.

The oldest residence on the island, the Coffin House is the only structure still standing from the original settlement on Nantucket. Jethro Coffin, for whom the saltbox home was a wedding gift, was grandson of Tristram Coffin, one of the original settlers of the island. The home has been restored but maintains much of its seventeenth-century feel. It is set back from the road across a beautiful grassy field, looking like a historic postcard. Behind the house is a kitchen garden complete with the sorts of herbs and vegetables that would have been grown here during the early 1700s.

The house is open for tours daily from around Memorial Day through Columbus Day. Admission: adults, $6; children, $3; under 6, free.

GPS: 41.286896,-70.102547

Directions: From the Oldest House continue down Sunset Hill Lane to W. Chester Street. Turn left on W. Chester, then bear right onto N. Centre Street. The next destination is immediately on the right. (Distance: 0.2 miles; Driving Time: 1 min.)

7. AMERICAN SEASONS
80 Centre Street

With a recent ownership change American Seasons is fully prepared to continue its tradition of great food and a great atmosphere. World-renowned chef Neil Ferguson bought the restaurant in 2015 from longtime owners Michael and Orla LaScola. Founded in 1988, American Seasons found its greatest era of prosperity under the LaScolas. Having been positively featured in publications such as *Food & Wine* and *Boston Magazine*, Ferguson has a tough act to follow but his experience in Paris, London, and New York should allay any fear from longtime patrons.

GPS: 41.286835,-70.102394

Directions: From American Seasons the next destination is right next door.

8. REGATTA INN
78 Centre Street

This Federal-style inn has eight rooms and a whole lot to be proud of. It was included in *Travel + Leisure*'s "World's Greatest Dream Trips" in 2014. Each of the rooms is brilliantly decorated and splendidly private. This inn seems to have everything one could want and more. Though a relative newbie to the island, having opened in 2013, this spot surely will be a popular destination for travelers for years to come.

9. THE CENTERBOARD INN
8 Chester Street

The sister inn of Regatta, this is a former whaling captain's home built in 1880. It was remodeled in 2012 by the new owners, Paul and Lauri Benk. What Centerboard gives its guests is a Victorian-era feel inside combined with modern amenities and great attention to detail. These things come together to make one of the highest rated bed & breakfasts on the island. On cool nights, relax around the firepit in an Adirondack chair.

GPS: 41.287945,-70.101059

Directions: From Centerboard Inn continue on Chester Street, which becomes Easton Street. Follow Easton for a few hundred feet; the next destination is on the left. (Distance: 500 feet; Driving Time: >1 min.)

10. NANTUCKET HOTEL & RESORT
77 Easton Street

Established in 1891, this famed resort has been routinely named one of the top destinations in the country. Known nearly as much for its antique fire engine and old green guest trolley, the Nantucket Hotel & Resort has been ahead of its time almost since the beginning. Originally known as "Point Breeze," this resort was completely renovated in 2012, updating and improving much while not losing its historic island roots. There are accommodations ranging from regular hotel rooms to premium four-bedroom suites for up to twelve people. Complete with a fitness club and restaurant, there is almost nothing one needs that the Nantucket Hotel does not have.

GPS: 41.287071,-70.101891

Directions: From the Nantucket Hotel head back up Chester Street, then take the first left onto Centre Street. The next destination is after a few hundred feet on the left. (Distance: 0.1 miles; Driving Time: 1 min.)

11. MARTIN HOUSE INN
61 Centre Street

Right in the heart of downtown, this is a beautiful spot to spend the night. The home was built in 1803 and after six generations of private ownership, it first became an inn in the 1920s under the name Wonoma Inn. It became known as the Martin House Inn in 1941. Outside and inside, this bed and breakfast manages to seamlessly mix the modern day in while not losing touch with the history that is so important to the people of Nantucket. Each of the eleven rooms are magnificently decorated. With treats like afternoon tea, this year-round locale makes a great base camp for an island trip.

FROM THE ROTARY BACK TO DOWNTOWN

12. FIRST CONGREGATIONAL CHURCH
62 Centre Street

This beautifully designed church was built in the early 1700s and sits atop Beacon Hill. For a small donation, one can climb to the top of the 120-foot-tall bell tower. The view from on high is breathtaking. Stretched before you is the harbor filled with boats, and from side to side you can see street after street of shops and historic homes.

The donation to the church upon entry is well worth the sights you will see from the top. Simply amazing.

FROM THE ROTARY BACK TO DOWNTOWN

GPS: 41.285212, -70.099942

Directions: From the church, continue along Centre Street, then take the third left onto Broad Street. The next destination is on the left. (Distance: 0.1 miles; Driving Time: 1 min.)

13. JARED COFFIN HOUSE
29 Broad Street

The first brick mansion built on the island, this was the homestead of one of the most successful ship owners during the height of the whaling industry on the island. The three-story building sits a short walk from the ferry docks and was instrumental in helping prevent the spread of the Great Fire that devastated the downtown area in 1846. The home was built in 1845, but it now features an addition, and it serves as a popular inn with thirty rooms. It's Federal-style architecture seems to fit in seamlessly among the other historic buildings that dot downtown Nantucket.

FROM THE ROTARY BACK TO DOWNTOWN

14. LE LANGUEDOC INN AND RESTAURANT
24 Broad Street

One of the top-rated restaurants on the island, Le Languedoc is as charming and delightful as it is unassuming. Established in 1976, this captivating French-cuisine locale has been run by the same people for thirty-five years and is named after a region in the south of France. The

location doubles as a cozy inn along with its sister inn, #3 Hussey Street Guest House. Despite its French connection, this bistro has favorites like Nantucket bay scallops and delicacies like Kobe beef. Stop in for lunch, dinner, or Sunday brunch. Open from mid-April through January 1.

GPS: 41.285347,-70.100235

Directions: From Le Languedoc continue (east) down Broad Street to the next destination.

15. THE BROTHERHOOD OF THIEVES
23 Broad Street

This is one historic spot among many on Broad Street. The name of the restaurant comes directly from an anti-slavery pamphlet written in 1844 by abolitionist Stephen S. Foster. The restaurant, established in 1972, looks to honor the ideals of historic Nantucket residents such as Foster, Maria Mitchell (a pioneer for women in astronomy; see page 67), and Benjamin Franklin-Folger (the island's first genealogist). The lower level of the restaurant is the original location and provides the look and feel of an 1840s whaling bar. It is this area that gives the Brotherhood a unique atmosphere and makes it a must for any visitor to the island.

GPS: 41.285358,-70.099983

Directions: From Brotherhood of Thieves continue (east) down Broad Street to the next destination.

16. 21 BROAD HOTEL
21 Broad Street

Only steps from the Steamboat Wharf ferry dock, 21 Broad is a new hotel that manages to look and feel as if it has been sitting in the center of town for decades. It caters to all types of travelers and is close to all of the shops and restaurants Nantucket is known for. There are twenty-seven rooms, each with modern yet classic style. Unique amenities like the Vitamin C shower make 21 Broad a spot that is sure to be a top destination for years to come. *Conde Nast Traveler* and *Food & Wine* have already proclaimed it as such.

17. DUNE RESTAURANT & BAR
20 Broad Street

Established in 2009, Dune is new to the Nantucket restaurant scene but has a known name behind the scenes. Their chef and owner Michael Getter had been associated with other locations on the island, including the highly rated American Seasons. His experience and creativity shine in this new spot. Dune prides itself as modern chic meets casual comfort. Zagat notes its "wonderful" and "light" atmosphere and the creations of the "imaginative" Getter. It is as beautifully unassuming on the outside as it is proudly comforting on the inside.

18. NANTUCKET WHALING MUSEUM
15 Broad Street

This spot is an obvious must-see for any and all visitors to the island. Nantucket was the whaling capital of the world in the eighteenth and early nineteenth centuries, and this museum attests to that history. The building itself was erected in 1848 for whale processing and now stands as a memory of the whaling history. Among the jewels of the museum are the original lens used to illuminate Sankaty Head Lighthouse in 1849 and a forty-six-foot-long skeleton of a sperm whale that washed up on shore in 1998. There is an extensive collection of whaling-era scrimshaw, clothing, and artwork. It does not have to be the first spot visited on Nantucket, but it needs to be on everybody's list.

The museum is open daily from mid-April through the end of October and with reduced hours in November, December, and March. It is closed January through mid-February. Admission: adults, $20; seniors and students, $18; children, ages 6–17, $5; under 6, free.

FROM THE ROTARY BACK TO DOWNTOWN

GPS: 41.286098,-70.099640

Directions: From the Whaling Museum head back up Broad Street, then take the first right onto N. Water Street. The next destination is a few hundred feet up on the right. (Distance: 500 feet; Driving Time: 1 min.)

19. THE PERIWINKLE BED & BREAKFAST
9 N. Water Street

On the cobblestones and in the midst of downtown is this peaceful place for relaxation. Each room is unique and lovingly decorated. There is a small, cozy sitting area in the back where the sounds of Nantucket fill the air. This Greek Revival–style inn fits the feel of the island while also boasting some necessary modern amenities such as flat-screen televisions and personal Keurig coffee makers in each room. Close to everything in downtown, this is a fine home base.

20. BRASS LANTERN INN
11 N. Water Street

Fifteen beautiful rooms in a terrific setting smack in the middle of historic downtown: What could be better? At Brass Lantern, you can also bring your favorite four-legged friend with you. That's right, this is one of the few pet-friendly inns on the island, and it operates from April through the beginning of December. With a garden, patio, and homemade granola for breakfast, this is also a popular choice as a wedding site. The original building burned during the Great Fire of 1846 with the current building relatively unchanged until the 1990s. The owners pride themselves on "simple pleasures in casual elegance," and they surely deliver.

GPS: 41.286373,-70.100624
Directions: From Brass Lantern Inn continue along N. Water Street, then take the first left onto Step Lane. The next destination is a few hundred feet up on the right. (Distance: 500 feet; Driving Time: <1 min.)

21. THE VERANDA HOUSE
3 Step Lane

This "retro-chic" inn built in 1864 prides itself on personal concierge service and sweeping harbor views. The many verandas give visitors tremendous views, while the amenities such as a gourmet continental breakfast, flat-screen televisions, and complimentary beach amenities give visitors all the comforts they could need on their island getaway. Each of the eighteen rooms at the Veranda House is elegant and modern. Many have their own private veranda to enhance your stay.

22. HARBORVIEW NANTUCKET
24 Washington Street

Eleven restored cottages located only a few blocks from the ferry make up this spectacular getaway. These historic cottages retain their classic Nantucket feel outside while giving visitors all of the modern amenities they need on the inside. With the cottages ranging from one to four bedrooms, there is a place for any size group here. Along with exceptional attention to detail, Harborview also specializes in green practices. These include using some recycled materials for the interiors and exteriors of cottages, water conservation, and energy efficiency. It is easy to see why this is such a popular place for visitors to call home while on the island.

23. THE COTTAGES & LOFTS AT THE BOAT BASIN
24 Old South Wharf

There are fabulous views aplenty at this dockside lodging powerhouse. While the cottages have the look outside of classic island fishing shacks, inside are incredible modern amenities. The cottages sit facing the boat basin, which during the high season is loaded with beautiful vessels. They also offer fishing experiences for children, which makes this a great family destination.

24. PROVISIONS
3 Harbor Square

On Straight Wharf, right on the water, Provisions is a popular sandwich spot. They are open seasonally and specialize in fresh breads and unique sandwiches. They have typical ingredients like turkey and ham but also dip into different territory with options like a Sicilian tuna sandwich or curried chicken salad. Stop in while and try as many of these as you can either while sitting inside or walking on the wharf. You can't go wrong.

25. JEWEL OF THE ISLE
6 Straight Wharf

This spot has been a mainstay on the island for more than a quarter-century, offering on-site repairs and unique jewelry. The Trainor family prides itself on coming up with many Nantucket designs for their handmade jewelry, including beautiful island-shaped pendants. Their daughter Meghan became a music sensation in 2014 when her first single, "All About That Bass," spent eight weeks at number-one on the Billboard charts. It is just another accolade for this well-respected island family and shop.

26. THE CLUB CAR
1 Main Street

This is quite literally a bar inside an old railroad car. This Nantucket institution opened in 1977 and has been enthralling visitors and locals alike ever since. The once-booming Nantucket Railroad was felled by World War I and a decline in riders. The Pullman car was all that remained of the former railroad station when the tracks were removed in 1917. The car became a successful diner, Allen's Lobster Grill and Diner, and remained such for forty years. If sitting in the railroad car is not appealing, there is an actual restaurant attached to it.

27. NOBBY CLOTHING SHOP
17 Main Street

One of the oldest businesses on the island, Nobby Clothing has been going strong since 1930. The Levine family is in its third generation of ownership and continues to be committed to the satisfaction of its customers. It is known for its Breton Reds, also known as Nantucket Reds, a style and color of pants commonly worn by islanders during the summer in place of khakis or chinos. The famed pants were featured in the 1980 book *The Official Preppy Handbook* and are inspired by cotton pants worn in Brittany, a region in the north of France. There is so much more to see at Nobby Clothing than just the Breton Reds though.

GPS: 41.283653,-70.098434

Directions: From Nobby Clothing continue up Main Street to the next destination on the right.

28. THE HUB OF NANTUCKET
31 Main Street

A popular coffee and meeting spot, The Hub is located smack-dab in the middle of the historic Main Street. Established in 1950, it offers all of the popular coffee drinks including espresso and cappuccino along with smoothies and teas. Their gift shop offers online sales, meaning one does not have to step foot on the island to have a little slice of Nantucket or The Hub (or, you can order those souvenirs you forgot to buy once you get home). But the buzz and ambience of this popular morning hangout should be enjoyed first-hand.

GPS: 41.283077,-70.099022

Directions: From The Hub continue up Main Street to the next destination on the left.

29. MITCHELL'S BOOK CORNER
54 Main Street

This is a fabulous independent bookstore that has been sharing the written word with customers on Nantucket since 1968. The times and books may have changed, but the classic atmosphere inside Mitchell's has not. The 1846 brick building became a bookstore thanks to Henry Mitchell Havemeyer and Mary Allen Sargent Havemeyer. It prides itself on having the largest collection of books on Nantucket, its whaling history, and genealogy. This along with its decades-old tradition of personalized service, makes Mitchell's the first stop for any vacationing reader.

30. MURRAY'S TOGGERY SHOP
62 Main Street

One of the oldest shops on the island, Murray's has been serving Nantucket since 1945. The Murray family has been running the business almost from the beginning. They carry the famed Nantucket Reds, the brand of "guaranteed to fade" pants commonly worn on the islands and Cape Cod during the summer. In addition to clothing the island for all four seasons for seven decades, Murray's also extends that family feel to its loyal customers. They pride themselves on satisfying patrons with service and a friendly chat as well.

GPS: 41.282494,-70.100487

Directions: From Murray's continue up Main Street a few hundred feet to the next destination on the left.

31. 76 MAIN STREET INN
76 Main Street

This inn is a beautiful place to stay on a beautiful section of Main Street. After a major renovation in 2013, it became a Best of Boston winner in 2014. The private courtyard is spectacular and might make you not even want to take the short walk downtown. Each of the rooms has also been renovated recently, so even if you have visited before it might be time to visit again.

GPS: 41.283789,-70.099878

Directions: From 76 Main head back down Main Street, turn left onto Centre Street, then take the first right onto India Street. The next destination is on the right at the intersection with Federal Street. (Distance: 0.2 miles; Driving Time: 1 min.)

32. SWEET INSPIRATIONS
0 India Ave.

This is one of the sweetest spots on the island, known for its chocolate-covered cranberries. Their first shop was opened in 1983, and they have been going strong ever since. There is something for everyone here but for those who cannot chose, it might be best to go with an assortment box. They recently moved from Centre Street back to their original home at the corner of India Avenue. A beautiful old-time handcrafted chocolate shop in the heart of Nantucket, this is a great place to stop for a snack or a gift.

33. NANTUCKET ATHENEUM
India Street

This amazing building is Nantucket's unique library. This spot played a big part in the pre-Civil War abolitionist movement as well. Many famed abolitionists such as William Lloyd Garrison, David Joy, Horace Greely, and a young Frederick Douglass spoke out against slavery here at various times.

The building became a library in 1900 but was a cultural center hosting lectures by acclaimed writers such as Ralph Waldo Emerson and Henry David Thoreau in the decades leading up to that change. This is so much more than just a unique piece of architecture where one can read and enjoy thousands of books. It is a large part of a greater history in this country that might be lost on the average visitor. There are also numerous genealogical and historical records for those wishing to trace their island roots as well.

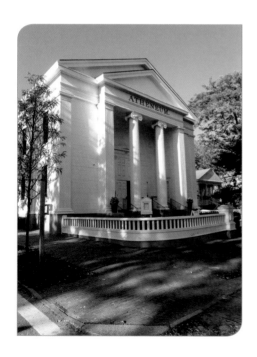

GPS: 41.284355,-70.097832

Directions: From the Atheneum head down Indian Street, then turn right onto S. Water Street. The next destination is straight ahead on the left. (Distance: 500 feet; Driving Time: <1 min.)

34. FOG ISLAND CAFÉ
7 S. Water Street

This is a delicious spot for breakfast and lunch, and for people-watching. Established in 1993 by husband-and-wife team Mark and Anne Dawson, there is no shortage of amazing dishes to try here. Whether it is a classic eggs Benedict for breakfast or turkey, cheddar, and avocado deli sandwich for lunch, it is appointment-eating at Fog Island.

35. LT. WAGNER MEMORIAL FOUNTAIN
Main Street

This fountain stands as an unofficial entrance to the shopping area of historic downtown Nantucket. The green-colored fountain is usually filled with flowers during the high season and is right in the middle of the legendary cobblestone streets. It is symbolic of the unique feeling and culture you experience downtown.

Though originally erected during the 1880s, this marker is now a memorial in tribute to Lt. Max Wagner, the only citizen of Nantucket to die during the Spanish-American War. The beautiful flowers are maintained by the Nantucket Garden Club.

36. NANTUCKET COMPASS ROSE MURAL
16 Main Street

This is a spot that thousands of visitors see and enjoy in historic downtown Nantucket. It is a quite simple compass rose showing the island where you stand as the center with many point of interest located all around it. It adorns the side of the Ralph Lauren store on Main Street.

The area where this mural is located is called Gardiner's Corner after photographer H. Marshall Gardiner, who came to the island in 1910 and created this incredible work of art in 1936. There are well-known localities placed around the rose such as Hong Kong, Spain, London, and Paris. The lesser-known spots like Mackinac Island in Michigan are nods to spots where Gardiner spent time during his childhood. It is a popular spot for photographs and deserves to be viewed by all passersby.

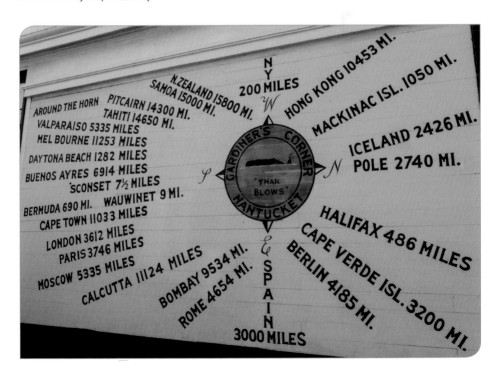

GPS: 41.284617, -70.098319

Directions: From the Compass Rose head west on Main Street, then take the first right onto Federal Street. Take the third right onto Oak Street, then take the first right onto S. Water Street. The next destination is on the left. (Distance: 0.2 miles; Driving Time: 1 min.)

37. DREAMLAND PERFORMING ARTS CENTER

17 S. Water Street

A former Quaker meetinghouse and host to abolitionist meetings, this spot has been an important part of Nantucket for more than 180 years. Before it came back to Water Street, this building had been disassembled and became a part of the Nantucket Hotel. It earned the name Dreamland Theatre in 1911, showing the latest moving pictures and hosting vaudeville entertainment. It has been Nantucket's premier entertainment destination for more than eighty years. The theatre was lovingly renovated over the past few years by the nonprofit Dreamland Foundation.

38. JOHNSTON'S OF ELGIN CASHMERE SHOP

4 Federal Street

This Nantucket shop has roots stretching more than 3,000 miles across the Atlantic and more than 200 years into the past. Known the world over for their cashmere, Johnston's home is in Scotland. Established in 1797, this giant began exporting its products across the globe in the 1860s, eventually finding a home on Nantucket. It is a unique story and journey. The clothing is well worth checking out.

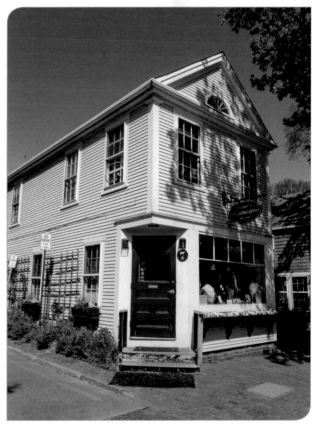

39. THE PEARL
12 Federal Street

Established in 1999, this hugely popular restaurant deserves its big reputation. Their Salt + Pepper Wok Fried Lobster is not only considered the best seafood dish on the island but was also given a "World's Best" recommendation from *Travel + Leisure*. The authentic Asian fare comes from Chef Seth Raynor, who spent time in Vietnam, Japan, and Thailand researching the local cuisines. Countless awards and stacks of positive reviews make The Pearl a spot that does not need to brag.

This is the end of our island tour of Nantucket. I hope that you have enjoyed every step and every moment on this beautiful and historic island. Come back anytime!

ACKNOWLEDGMENTS

Thank you to . . .

Mom & Dad, Kate, Lindsay, Ashley, Kaleigh, Emma, Liam, Landon, Lucas, Nina & Grampa, my aunts, uncles, and cousins, too many to name.

Emily, Steve, Deanna & Michael, Meg, Judy, Rob, DJW, Mike & Barb's Bikes in Dennis, Monique, Maui, Debbie and the Clark family

My good friend Bill DeSousa-Mauk, the Steamship Authority, and the great people at the Nantucket Chamber.

Inside the First Congregational Church

BIBLIOGRAPHY

Resources consulted for the book include the websites of the many organizations and businesses mentioned. Of particular interest for the visitor to Nantucket are these sources.

Douglas-Lithgow, Robert Alesander. *Nantucket: A History*. New York: G.P. Putnam's Sons, 1914. Accessed through Google Books.

Egan Maritime Institute (Nantucket *Shipwreck & Lifesaving Museum*). www.nantucketshipwreck.org.

Green, Eugene, and William L. Sachse. *Names of the Land: Cape Cod, Nantucket, Martha's Vineyard, and the Elizabeth Islands.* Chester, CT: Globe Pequot, 1983.

"Hardship and Courage." *Cape Cod Times*, March 6, 2003. http://www.capecodtimes.com/article/20030316/NEWS01/303169977&cid=sitesearch.

Maria Mitchell Association, www.mariamitchell.org.

Museum of African American History, Boton and Nantucket, www.afroammuseum.org.

"Nantucket Cliff Range Lighthouse." Lighthousefriends.com.

Nantucket Conservation Foundation. www.nantucketconservation.org.

Nantucket Historical Association. http://nha.org/index.html.

Nantucket Regional Transit Authority. http://www.nrtawave.com.

New England Lighthouses: A Virtual Guide. www.newenglandlighthouses.net.

Yesterday's Island/Today's Nantucket. nantucket.net.

INDEX